With God's love,
Kathy O'Neil
2015

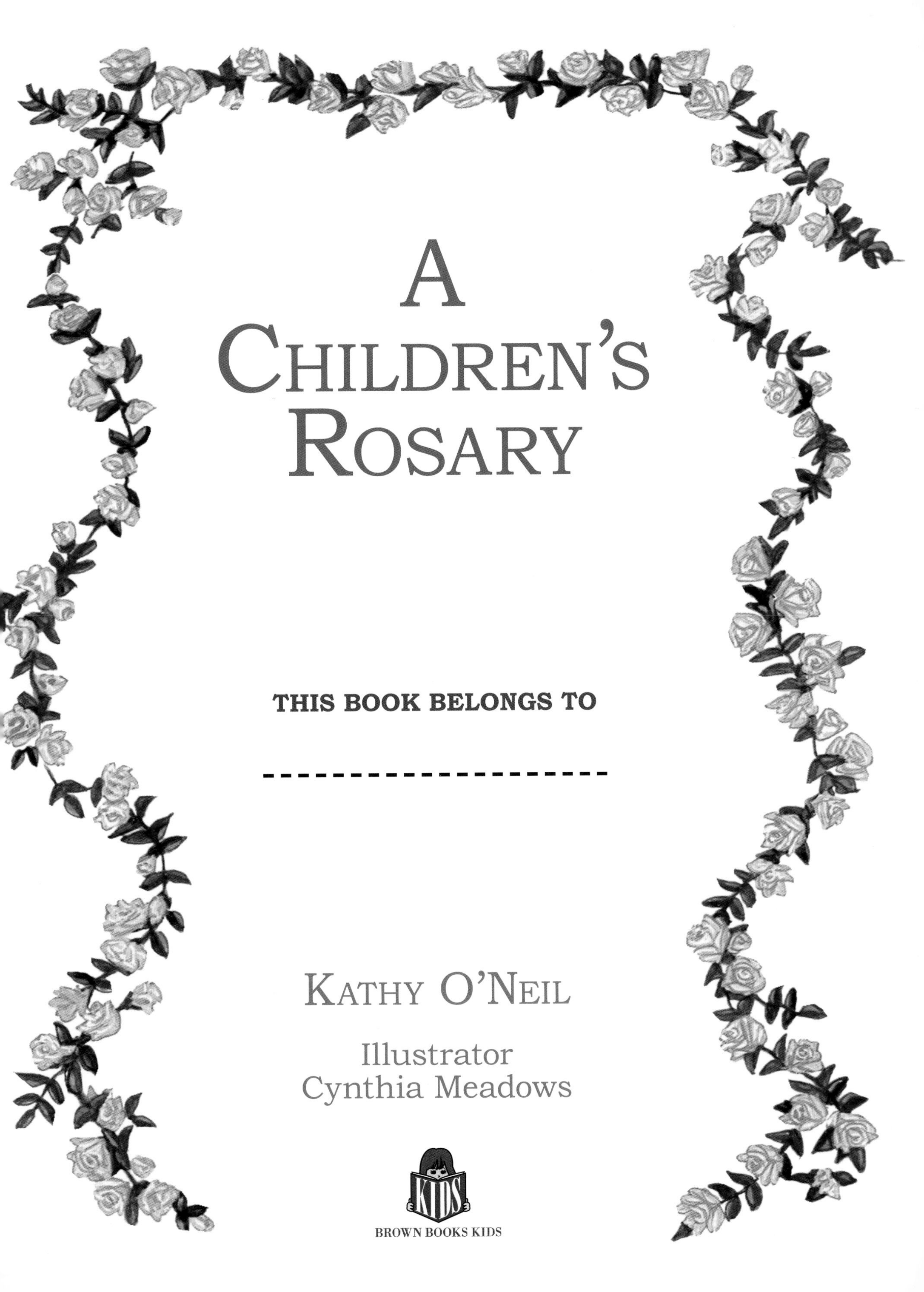

A Children's Rosary

THIS BOOK BELONGS TO

KATHY O'NEIL

Illustrator
Cynthia Meadows

BROWN BOOKS KIDS

A Children's Rosary

Brown Books Kids
16250 Knoll Trail Drive, Suite 205
Dallas, Texas 75248
www.BrownBooksKids.com
(972) 381-0009

A New Era in Publishing™

ISBN 978-1-61254-170-9
LCCN 2014937197

Printed in the United States
10 9 8 7 6 5 4 3 2 1

For more information or to contact the author, please go to www.AChildrensRosary.com

NIHIL OBSTAT Jonathan Wallis, S.T.L.
Censor Librorum

IMPRIMATUR + Michael Fors Olson, S.T.D.
Bishop of Fort Worth

Fort Worth, TX, April 3, 2014

DEDICATION

This book is dedicated to my mother, who cherishes the rosary and her Catholic faith.

I also dedicate this book to Grandad, who has created beautiful rosaries for countless numbers of children and adults for many years. Thank you, Grandad, for always having a rosary in your pocket.

ACKNOWLEDGMENTS

Many thanks to the St. Andrew's Friars for conducting a prayer check for me.

Tommy, I have to thank you also. If you had not injured your hand in football and had surgery on it, I may never have conceived this book while I sat and anxiously waited for Dr. Wroten to assure your dad and me that you were all right.

And thank you most of all to Jim for believing in me.

INTRODUCTION

There are so many different forms of prayer that we can use to talk and to listen to God. Can you just imagine how happy he is when he hears our voices, and he listens to our hearts? Praying the rosary is a special way of talking to God, Jesus, Mary, and the Saints—all at the same time. Wow!

Many people have forgotten how to pray the rosary, and some have never been taught how to pray it. Maybe even some adults you might know have never learned it. This book will help you and the people you love learn how to pray the rosary and open your hearts to Mary's love. Never forget that Jesus and Mary love you very much.

Kathy O'Neil

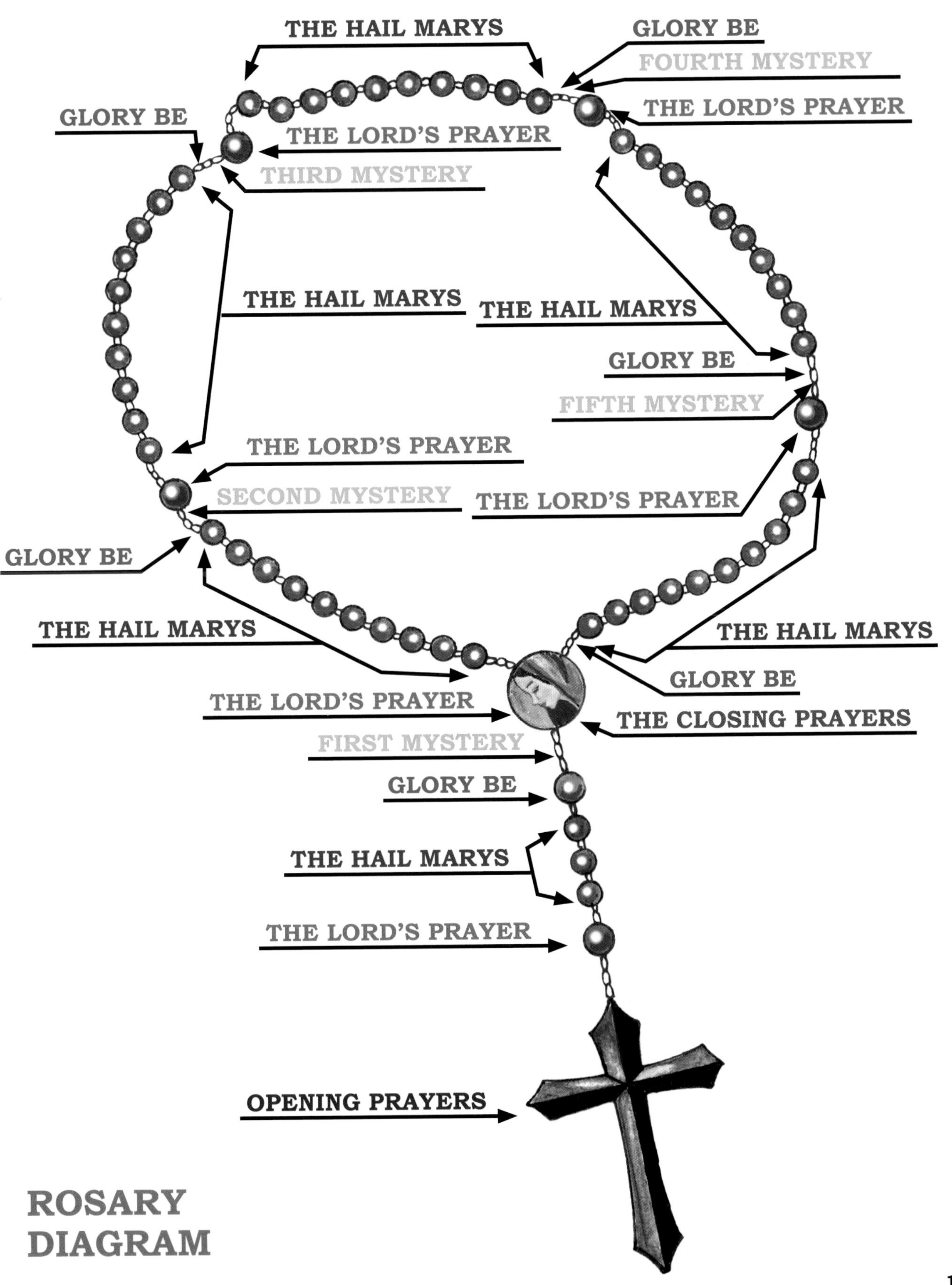

ROSARY DIAGRAM

OPENING PRAYERS

THE SIGN OF THE CROSS

In the name of the Father, and of the Son, and of the Holy Spirit.

Amen.

THE APOSTLES' CREED

I believe in God, the Father almighty, Creator of heaven and earth, and in Jesus Christ, his only Son, our Lord, who was conceived by the Holy Spirit, born of the Virgin Mary, suffered under Pontius Pilate, was crucified, died and was buried; he descended into hell; on the third day he rose again from the dead; he ascended into heaven, and is seated at the right hand of God the Father almighty; from there he shall come to judge the living and the dead.

I believe in the Holy Spirit, the holy Catholic Church, the communion of saints, the forgiveness of sins, the resurrection of the body, and life everlasting.

Amen.

THE LORD'S PRAYER

Our Father, who art in heaven,
hallowed be thy name;
thy kingdom come;
thy will be done on earth as it is in heaven.
Give us this day our daily bread;
and forgive us our trespasses
as we forgive those who trespass against us;
and lead us not into temptation,
but deliver us from evil.
Amen.

THE HAIL MARY

Hail Mary, full of grace, the Lord is with thee;
blessed art thou among women,
and blessed is the fruit of thy womb, Jesus.
Holy Mary, Mother of God,
pray for us sinners
now and at the hour of our death.
Amen.

GLORY BE

Glory be to the Father, and to the Son, and to the Holy Spirit. As it was in the beginning, is now, and ever shall be, world without end.
Amen.

CLOSING PRAYERS

HAIL HOLY QUEEN

Hail, holy Queen, Mother of mercy,
our life, our sweetness, and our hope.
To you do we cry, poor banished children of Eve;
to you do we send up our sighs,
mourning and weeping in this valley of tears.
Turn then, most gracious advocate,
your eyes of mercy toward us;
and after this, our exile,
show unto us the blessed fruit of your womb, Jesus.
O clement, O loving, O sweet Virgin Mary.
(Verse)
Pray for us, O Holy Mother of God,
(Response)
That we may be made worthy of the promises of Christ.

LET US PRAY

O God, whose only begotten Son, by his life, death, and resurrection has purchased for us the rewards of eternal life, grant, we beseech Thee, that meditating upon these mysteries of the Most Holy Rosary of the Blessed Virgin Mary, we may imitate what they contain, and obtain what they promise, through the same Christ our Lord.

Amen.

THE SIGN OF THE CROSS

In the name of the Father, and of the Son, and of the Holy Spirit.

Amen.

EASY TO FOLLOW INSTRUCTIONS

You may have noticed the colorful prayers in the front pages of your book. These prayers are color coded to match the different parts of the rosary. There are four sets of mysteries in the rosary so the book is divided into four sections:

- The Joyful Mysteries
- The Luminous Mysteries
- The Sorrowful Mysteries
- The Glorious Mysteries

All you need to do is follow the bead colors on the illustrations as you turn each page. Match the colors on your rosary illustrations to the colorful prayers in your book. In this way, following the colors is like following a map—a prayer map!

Each time you say the rosary, read and contemplate the mysteries where you see them written. You might even notice the beautiful illustrations as you go along.

Now if you are ready to try, then let's get going. You may need help from an adult the first time, but soon you will be able to follow the rosary on your own. Start the Joyful Mysteries of the rosary on the next page.

First Joyful Mystery

THE ANNUNCIATION

The Angel Gabriel tells Mary that she will have a baby and name him Jesus.

Second Joyful Mystery

THE VISITATION

When Elizabeth is visited by Mary, Elizabeth feels her own baby kick inside of her womb, and she is overjoyed.

THIRD JOYFUL MYSTERY

THE NATIVITY

Jesus is born in a stable and wrapped in swaddling clothes. That is why we celebrate Christmas!

Fourth Joyful Mystery

THE PRESENTATION

Mary and Joseph present baby Jesus in the temple.

Fifth Joyful Mystery

FINDING THE CHILD JESUS IN THE TEMPLE

Mary and Joseph are so happy to find young Jesus in the temple after searching for him for several days.

First Luminous Mystery

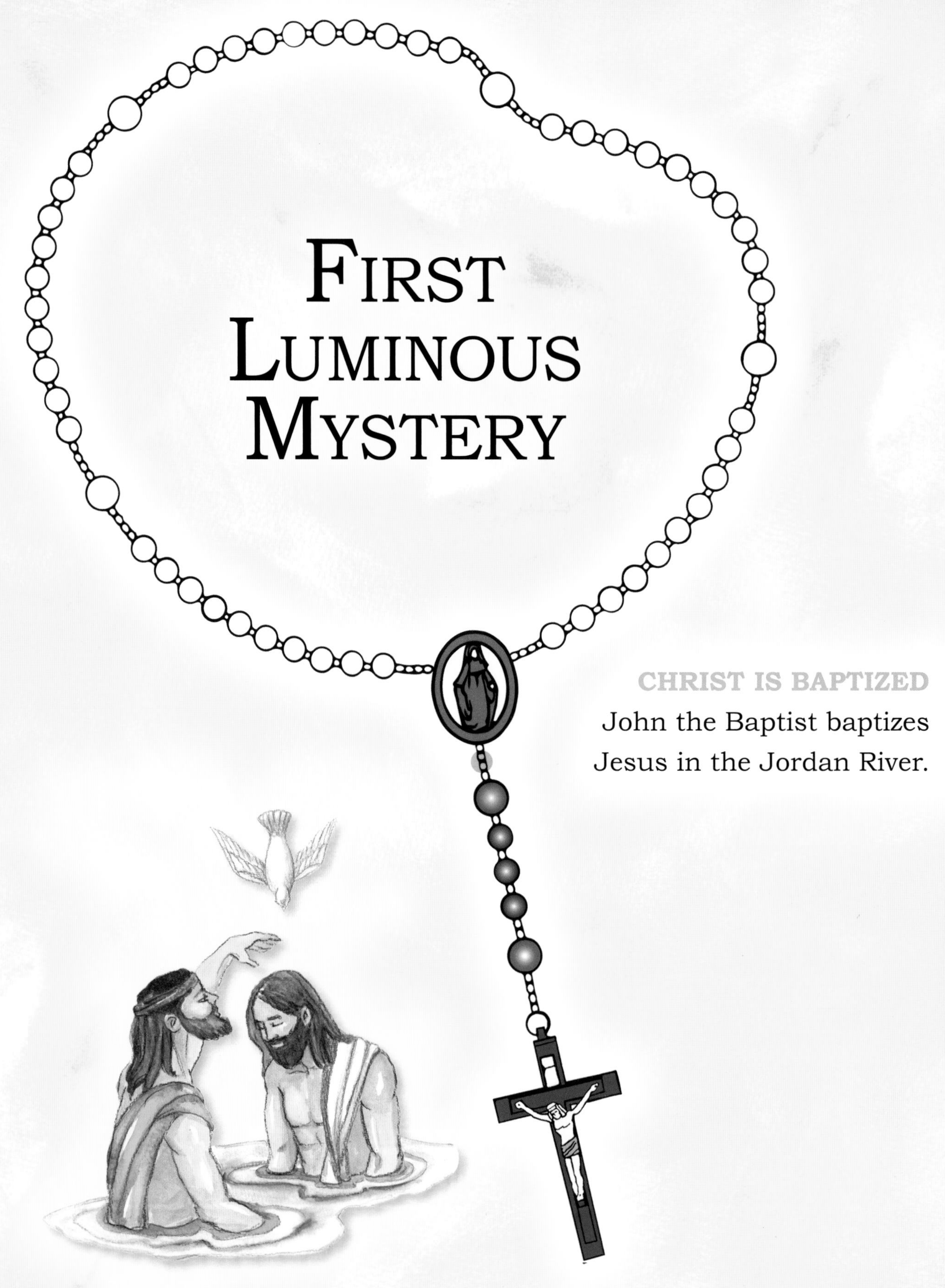

CHRIST IS BAPTIZED

John the Baptist baptizes
Jesus in the Jordan River.

Second Luminous Mystery

THE WEDDING AT CANA

After Mary asks, Jesus changes water to wine at the wedding reception.

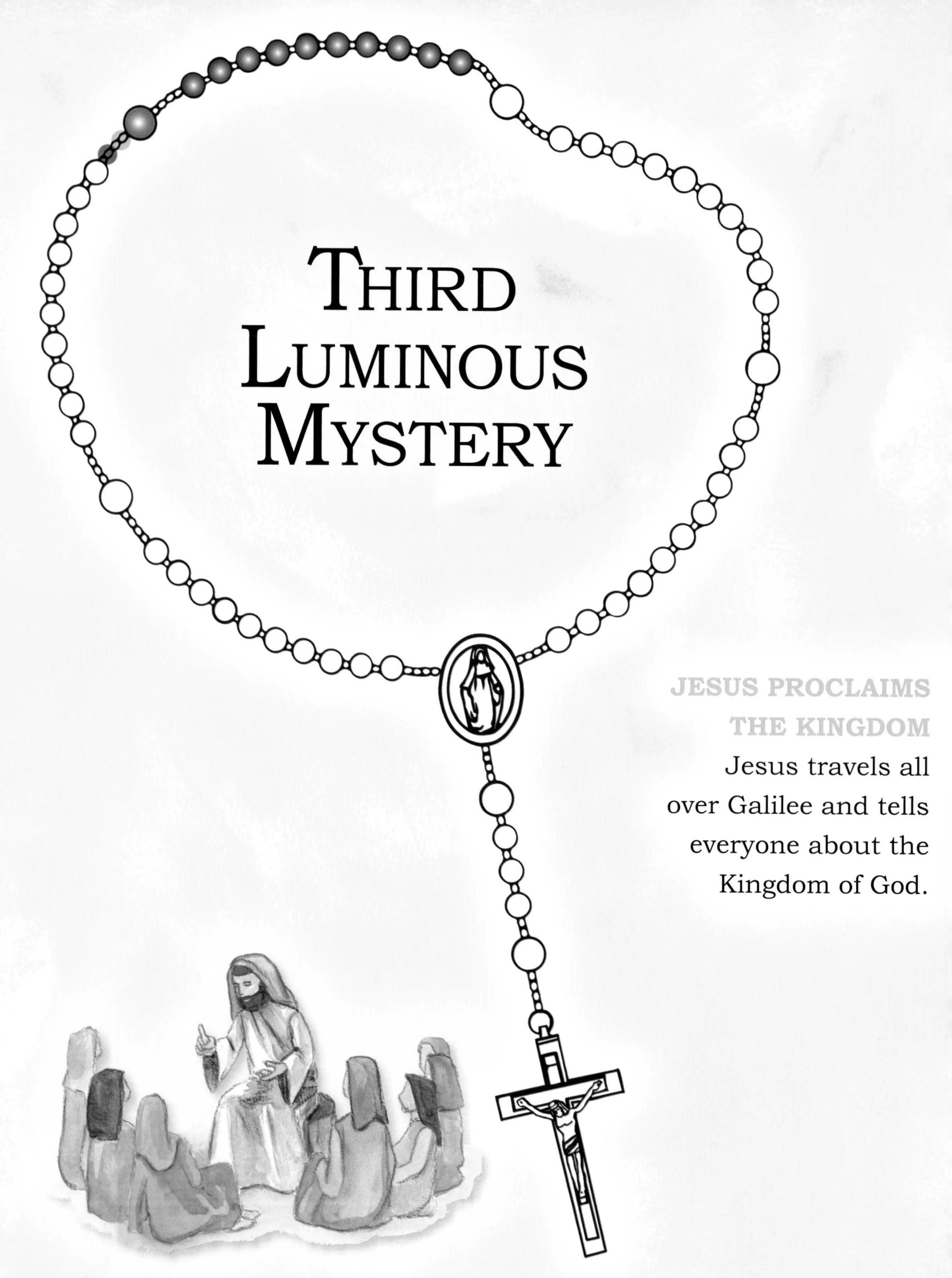

Third Luminous Mystery

JESUS PROCLAIMS THE KINGDOM

Jesus travels all over Galilee and tells everyone about the Kingdom of God.

FOURTH LUMINOUS MYSTERY

THE TRANSFIGURATION OF JESUS

While Jesus is praying, his face changes and his clothes become dazzling white.

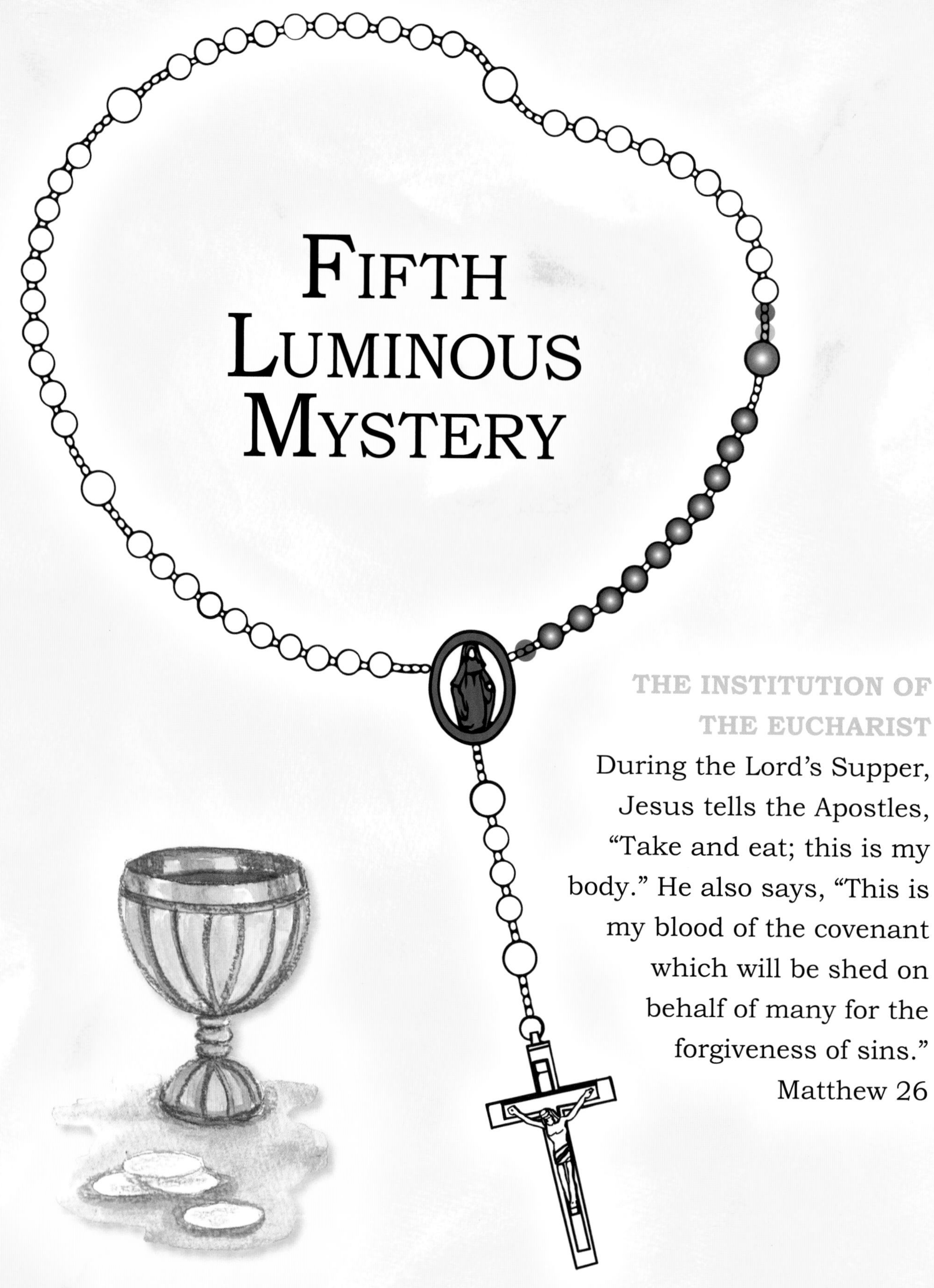

Fifth Luminous Mystery

THE INSTITUTION OF THE EUCHARIST

During the Lord's Supper, Jesus tells the Apostles, "Take and eat; this is my body." He also says, "This is my blood of the covenant which will be shed on behalf of many for the forgiveness of sins."
Matthew 26

FIRST SORROWFUL MYSTERY

THE AGONY IN THE GARDEN

Jesus is scared and sad in the Garden of Gethsemane as he prays to God.

Second Sorrowful Mystery

THE SCOURGING AT THE PILLAR

The soldiers whip and beat Jesus.

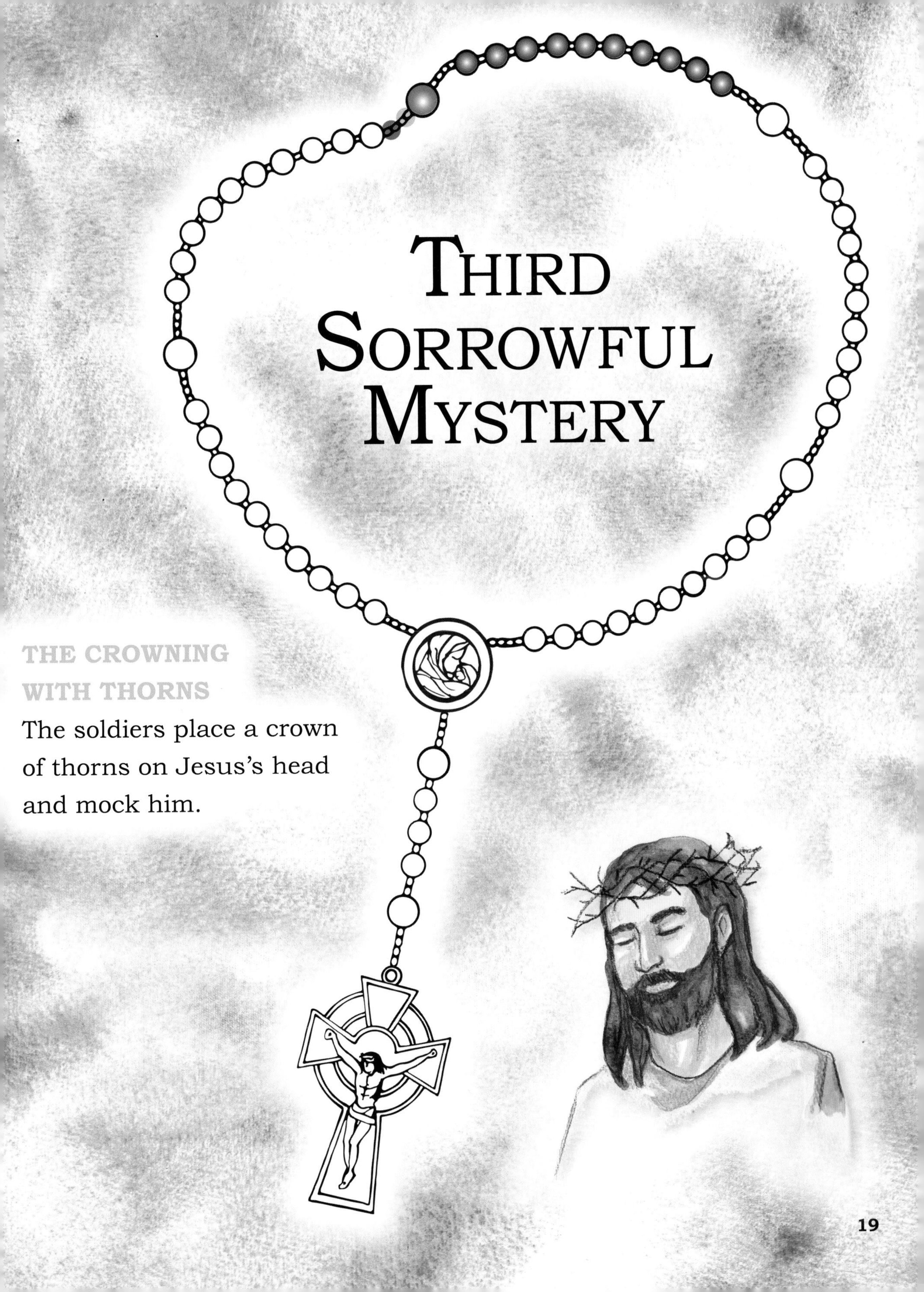

Third Sorrowful Mystery

THE CROWNING WITH THORNS

The soldiers place a crown of thorns on Jesus's head and mock him.

Fourth Sorrowful Mystery

THE CARRYING OF THE CROSS

Jesus has to carry his cross to Golgotha where he will be crucified.

FIFTH SORROWFUL MYSTERY

THE CRUCIFIXION

Jesus dies on the cross for us. Thank you, Jesus, for loving us so much.

First Glorious Mystery

THE RESURRECTION

After three days in the tomb, Jesus rises from the dead. That is why we celebrate Easter!

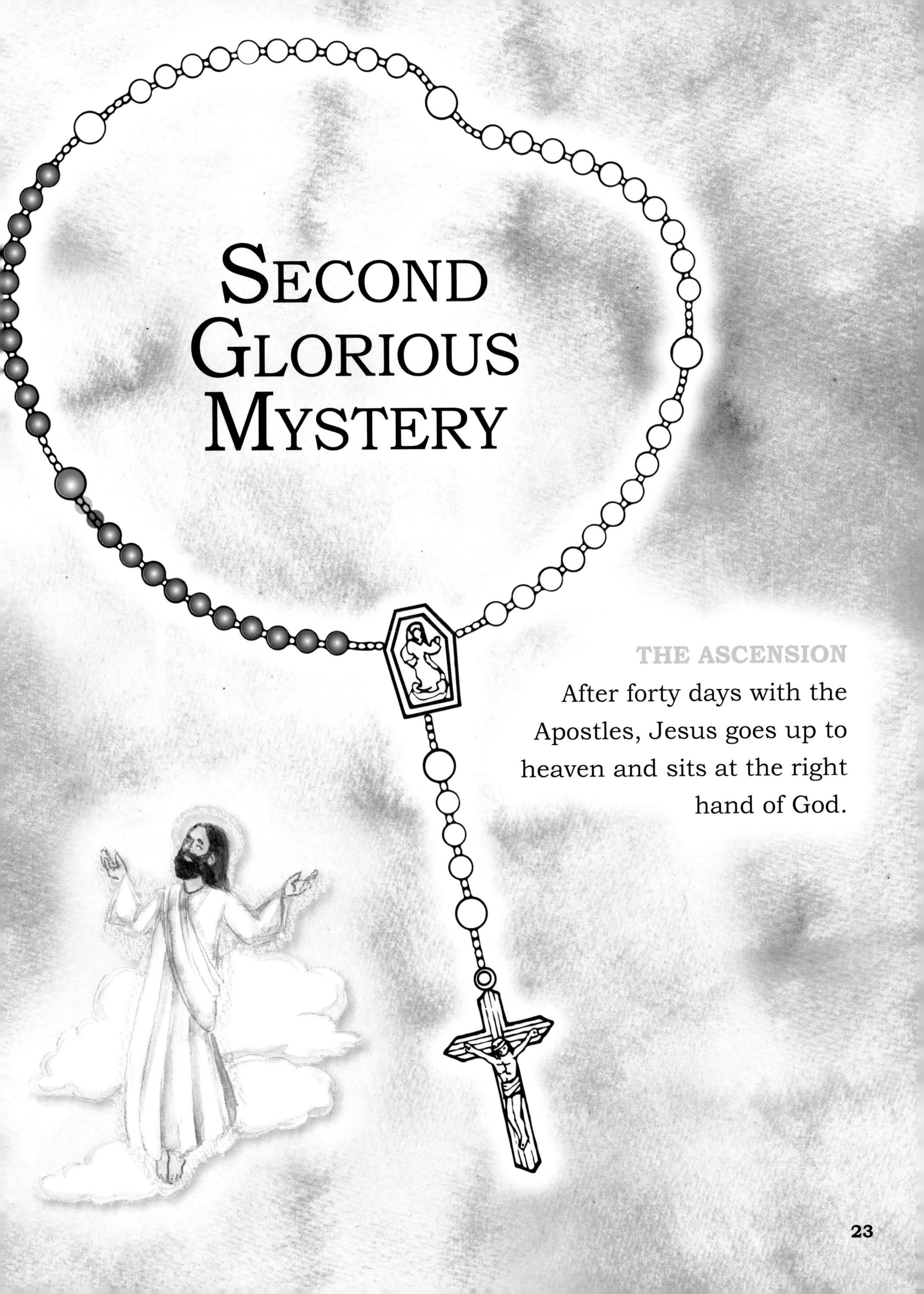

SECOND GLORIOUS MYSTERY

THE ASCENSION

After forty days with the Apostles, Jesus goes up to heaven and sits at the right hand of God.

Third Glorious Mystery

THE DESCENT OF THE HOLY SPIRIT

When the Apostles and Mary are together in a large room, Jesus sends the Holy Spirit over them like tongues of fire! The Holy Spirit gives them the wisdom and courage to spread the good news about God.

Fourth Glorious Mystery

THE ASSUMPTION

Mary is taken up to heaven to be with Jesus.

FIFTH GLORIOUS MYSTERY

THE CROWNING OF THE BLESSED VIRGIN MARY

Mary is crowned in heaven with a beautiful crown of twelve stars. She is clothed with the sun and the moon under her feet.

DAILY ROSARY PRAYER SCHEDULE

Jesus and Mary are always happy when you pray, and you may choose to pray whichever set of mysteries you would like. You do not need to finish the entire rosary at once. You may do just a little at a time. If you would like to follow a schedule, consider following the daily rosary schedule listed below.

SUNDAY	GLORIOUS MYSTERIES
MONDAY	JOYFUL MYSTERIES
TUESDAY	SORROWFUL MYSTERIES
WEDNESDAY	GLORIOUS MYSTERIES
THURSDAY	LUMINOUS MYSTERIES
FRIDAY	SORROWFUL MYSTERIES
SATURDAY	JOYFUL MYSTERIES

ABOUT THE AUTHOR—KATHY O'NEIL

Kathy O'Neil was born in Houston, Texas, and raised along with two sisters and two brothers. Kathy began teaching Sunday school and playing guitar at mass while in high school. Her interest in the rosary began many years ago when the Hail Mary and the Our Father became her go to prayers during times of stress, fear, relaxation, joy—really any time of the day! Her use of the rosary brings peace and joy to her heart. Kathy and her husband have raised four sons together in a busy, noisy, fun- and pet-filled home.

ABOUT THE ILLUSTRATOR—CYNTHIA MEADOWS

Cynthia Meadows, a native Texan, draws and paints on anything she can find due to her passion to decorate and color the world. Whether it is cartoons on the sides of her homework in elementary school, paintings as Christmas gifts, murals or faux finishes on walls, or illustrations and storyboards for advertising agencies, she continually decorates the world. Cynthia's desire to look inside characters is why she loves to illustrate children's books, to create characters, and to give the reader a positive—sometimes humorous—view of life. God, beauty, and imagination are important elements in Cynthia's life and work. She believes this wonderful rosary book will bring readers a more clear understanding of the rosary and the comfort and peace of God.